EASY BROADWAY
DUETS 2

8 EXCITING ARRANGEMENTS

BY GLENDA AUSTIN, ERIC BAUMGARTNER
NAOKO IKEDA, AND CAROLYN MILLER

ISBN 978-1-70515-824-1

EXCLUSIVELY DISTRIBUTED BY

Visit Hal Leonard Online at
www.halleonard.com

Contact us:
Hal Leonard
7777 West Bluemound Road
Milwaukee, WI 53213
Email: info@halleonard.com

In Europe, contact:
Hal Leonard Europe Limited
42 Wigmore Street
Marylebone, London, W1U 2RN
Email: info@halleonardeurope.com

In Australia, contact:
Hal Leonard Australia Pty. Ltd.
4 Lentara Court
Cheltenham, Victoria, 3192 Australia
Email: info@halleonard.com.au

Lullaby of Broadway

SECONDO

Words by Al Dubin
Music by Harry Warren
Arranged by Eric Baumgartner

Lullaby of Broadway

PRIMO

Words by Al Dubin
Music by Harry Warren
Arranged by Eric Baumgartner

Come on a-long and   lis-ten to ____   the lul-la-by of Broad-way...

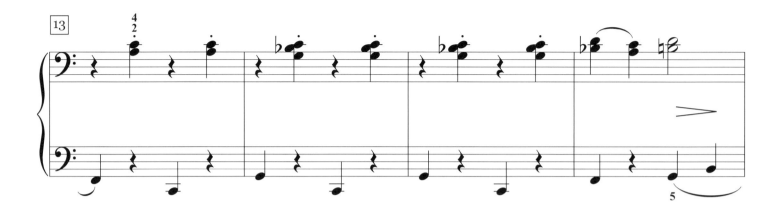

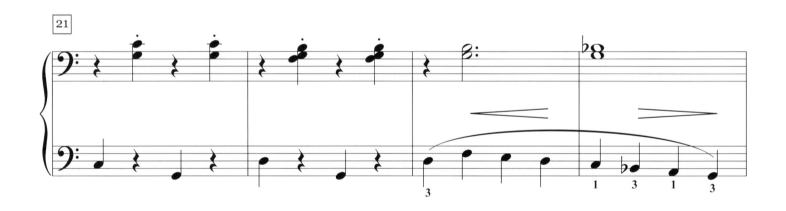

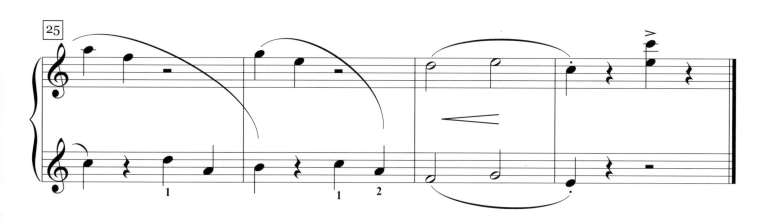

You'll Be Back

from HAMILTON

SECONDO

Words and Music by
Lin-Manuel Miranda
Arranged by Naoko Ikeda

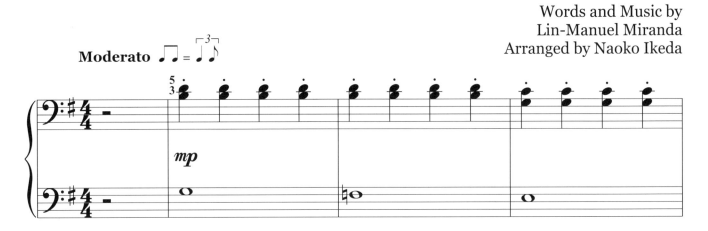

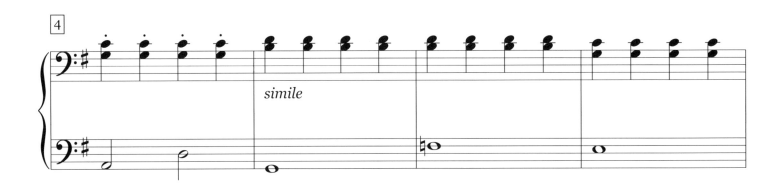

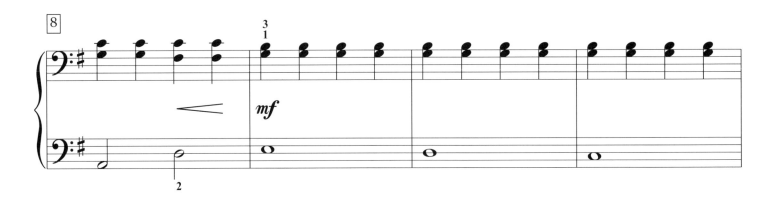

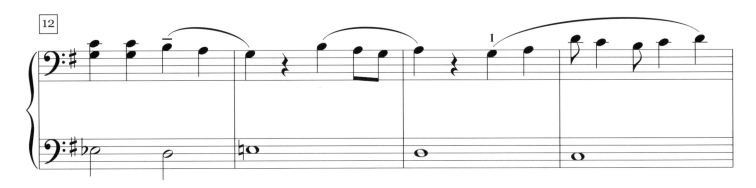

You'll Be Back

from HAMILTON

PRIMO

Words and Music by
Lin-Manuel Miranda
Arranged by Naoko Ikeda

SECONDO

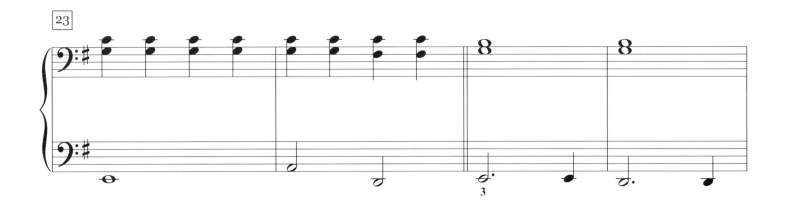

Da da da dat   da...

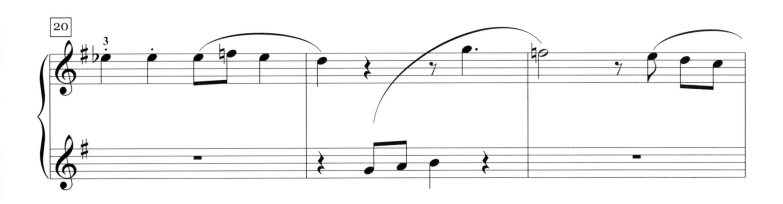

SECONDO

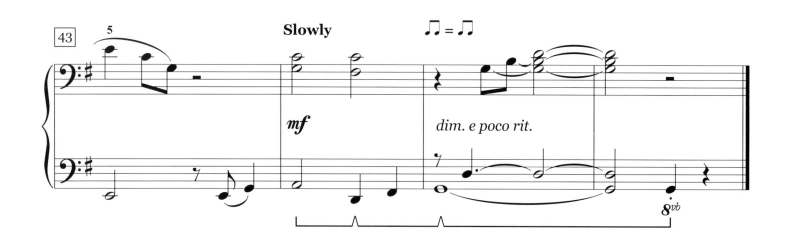

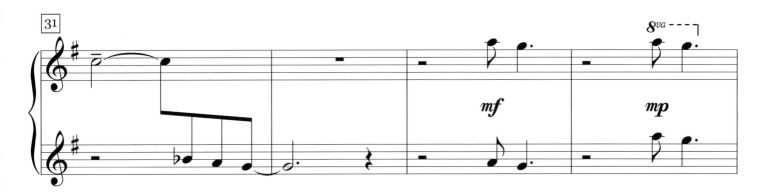

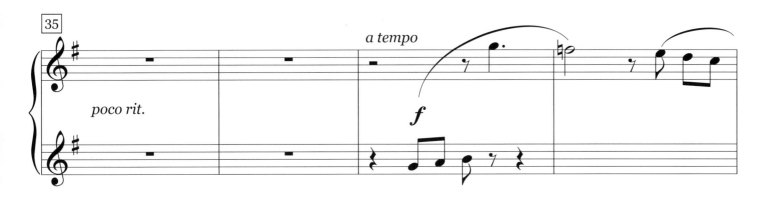

Jellicle Songs for Jellicle Cats

from CATS

SECONDO

Music by Andrew Lloyd Webber
Text by Trevor Nunn
and Richard Stilgoe after T.S. Eliot
Arranged by Eric Baumgartner

Jellicle Songs for Jellicle Cats

from CATS

PRIMO

Music by Andrew Lloyd Webber
Text by Trevor Nunn
and Richard Stilgoe after T.S. Eliot
Arranged by Eric Baumgartner

Playfully

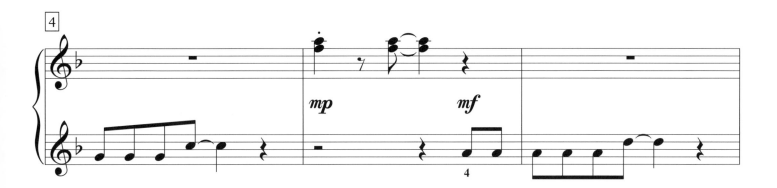

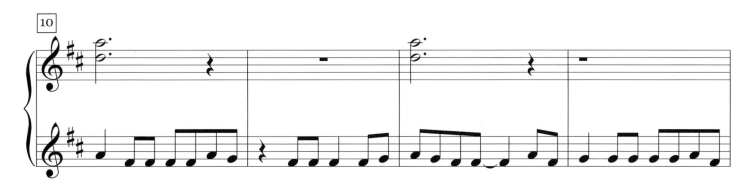

SECONDO

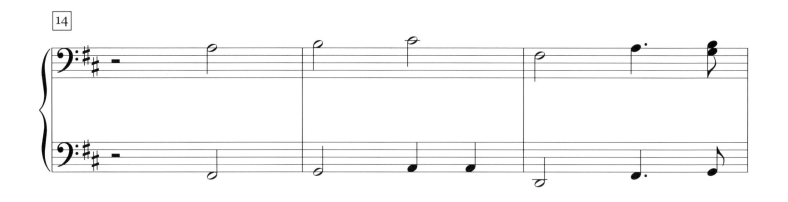

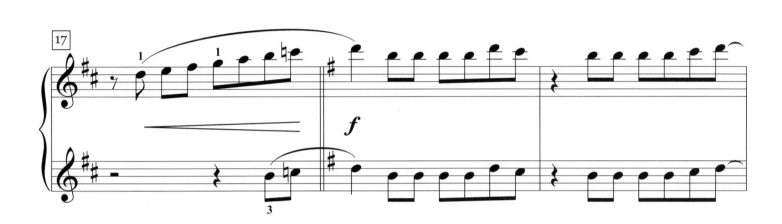

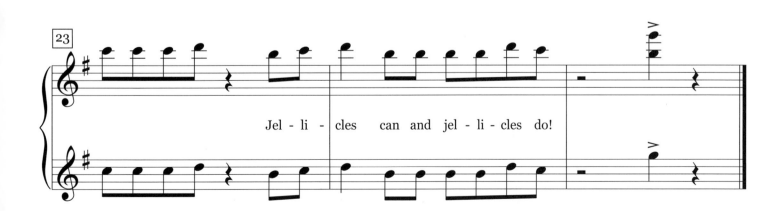

Jel - li - cles   can and jel - li - cles   do!

You Will Be Found

from DEAR EVAN HANSEN

SECONDO

Music and Lyrics by Benj Pasek
and Justin Paul
Arranged by Glenda Austin

Gently flowing

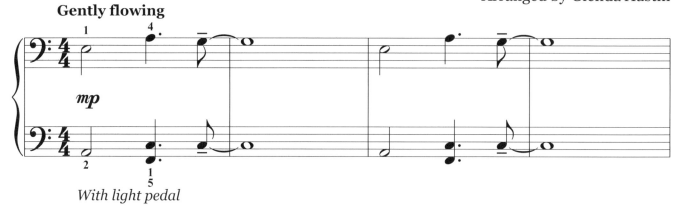

With light pedal

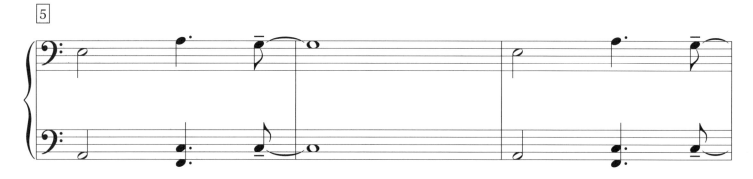

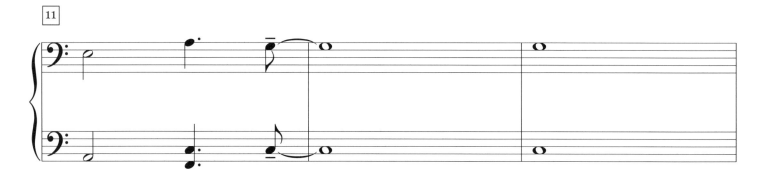

You Will Be Found
from DEAR EVAN HANSEN

PRIMO

Music and Lyrics by Benj Pasek
and Justin Paul
Arranged by Glenda Austin

Gently flowing

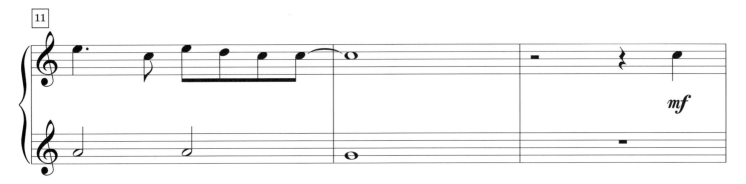

SECONDO

PRIMO

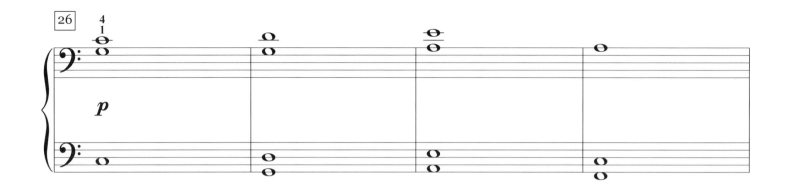

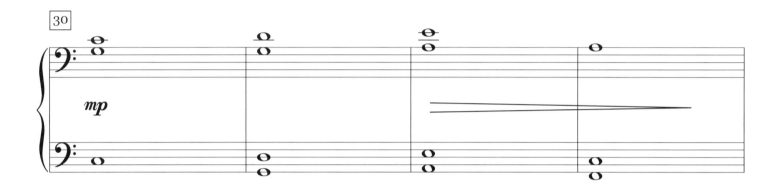

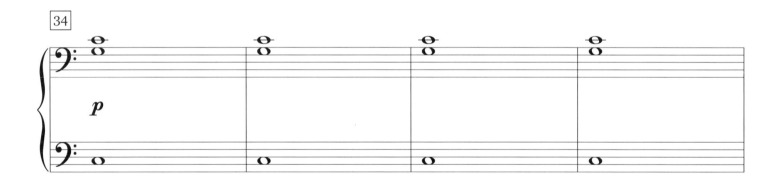

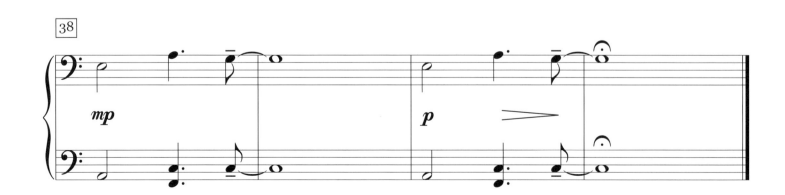

...You will be found. _____

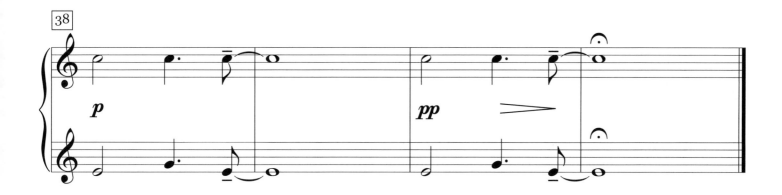

I Have Confidence
from THE SOUND OF MUSIC

SECONDO

Lyrics and Music by
Richard Rodgers
Arranged by Naoko Ikeda

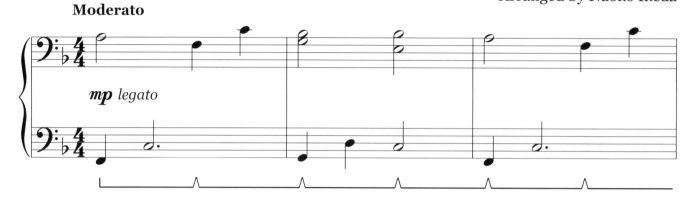

I Have Confidence
from THE SOUND OF MUSIC

PRIMO

Lyrics and Music by
Richard Rodgers
Arranged by Naoko Ikeda

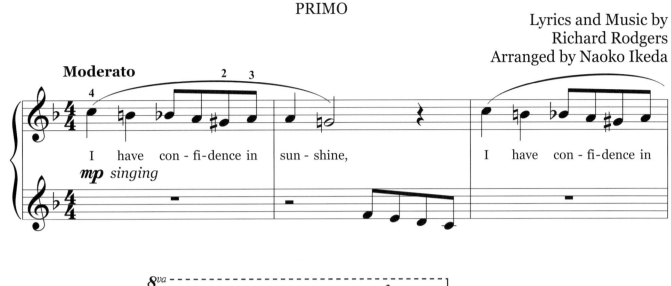

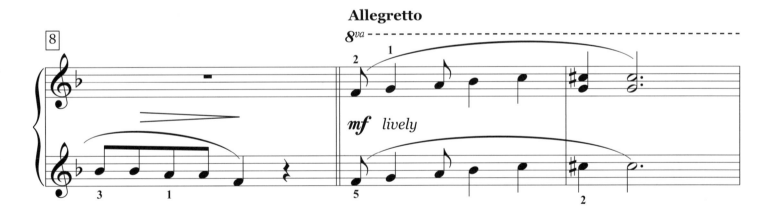

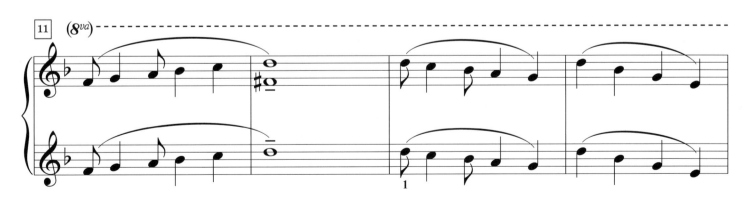

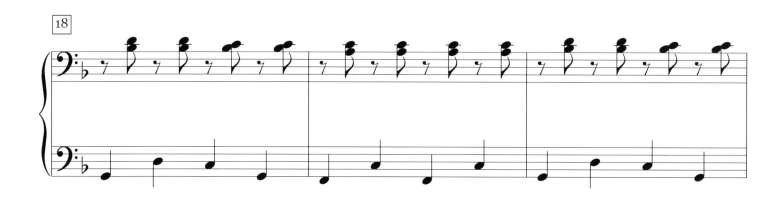

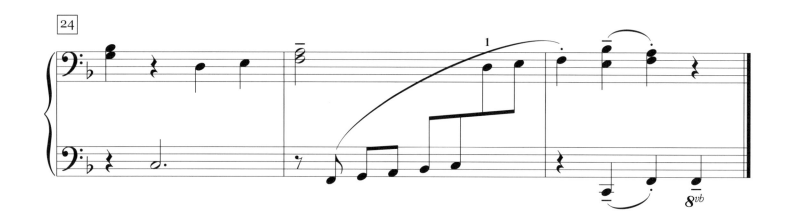

PRIMO

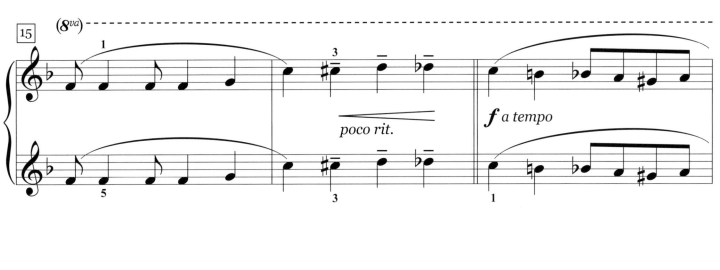

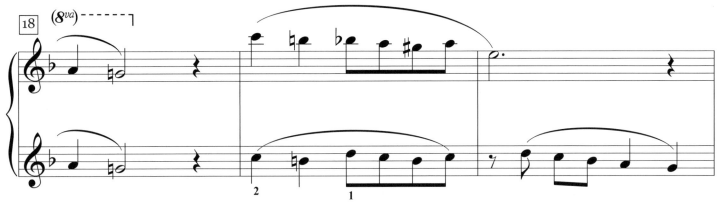

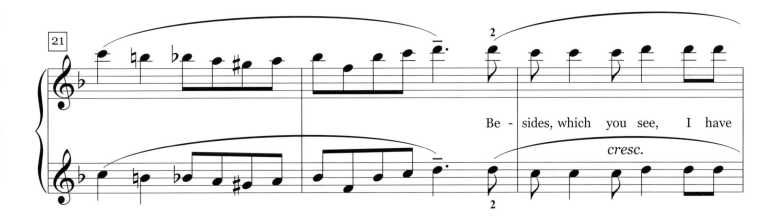

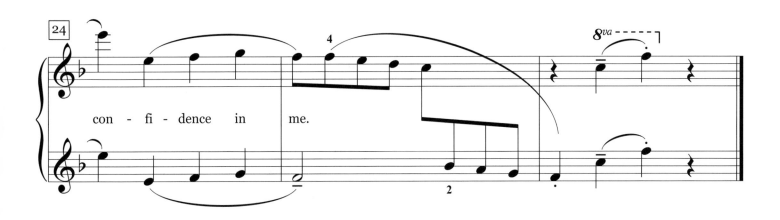

One
from A CHORUS LINE

SECONDO

Music by Marvin Hamlisch
Lyric by Edward Kleban
Arranged by Glenda Austin

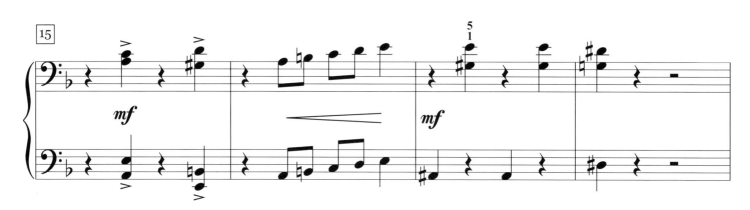

One
from A CHORUS LINE

PRIMO

Music by Marvin Hamlisch
Lyric by Edward Kleban
Arranged by Glenda Austin

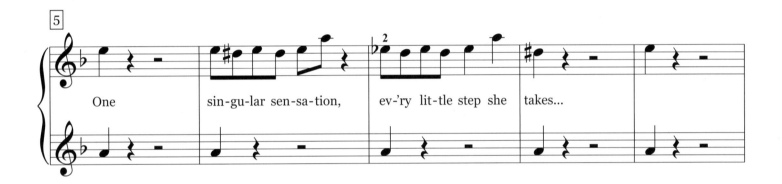

One — sin-gu-lar sen-sa-tion, ev-'ry lit-tle step she takes...

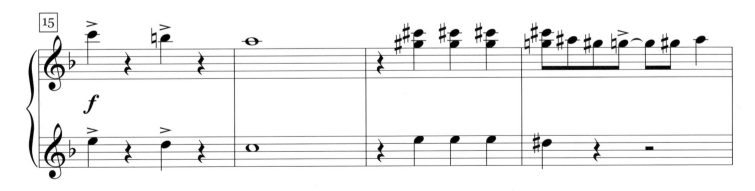

SECONDO

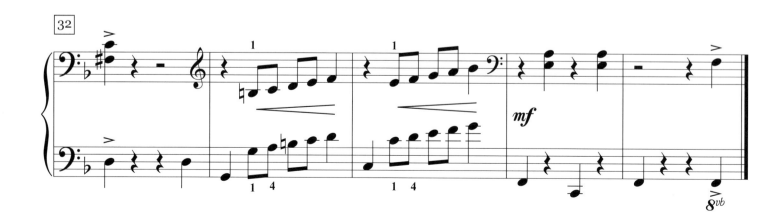

PRIMO

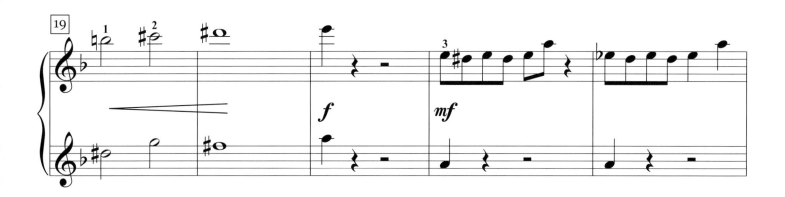

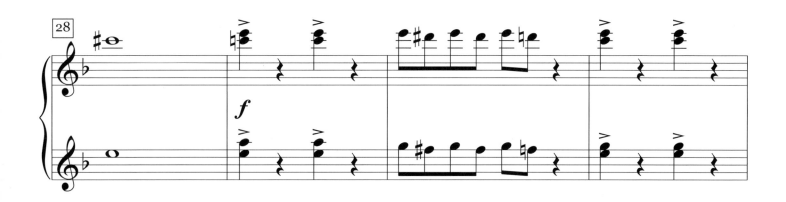

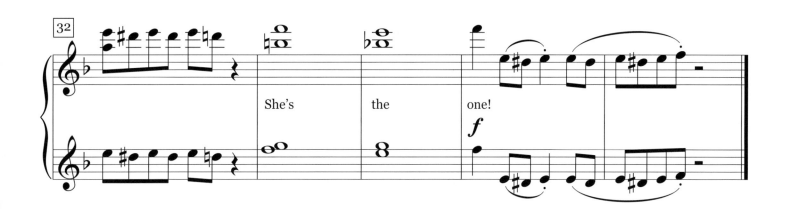

She's   the   one!

Popular
from the Broadway Musical WICKED

SECONDO

Music and Lyrics by
Stephen Schwartz
Arranged by Carolyn Miller

Bright and bubbly, with a lilt

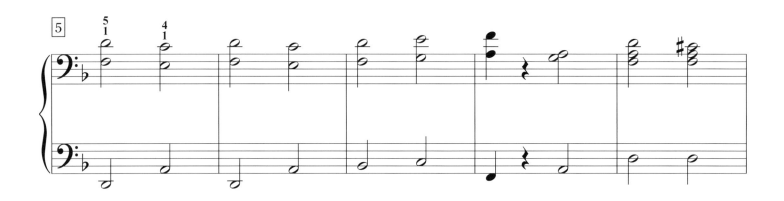

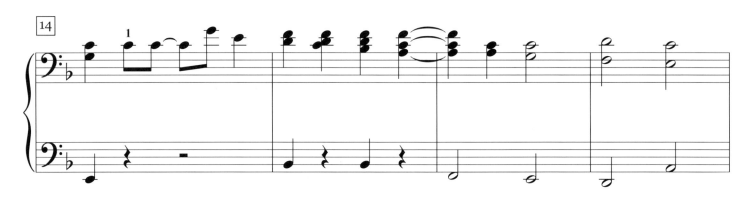

Popular
from the Broadway Musical WICKED

PRIMO

Music and Lyrics by
Stephen Schwartz
Arranged by Carolyn Miller

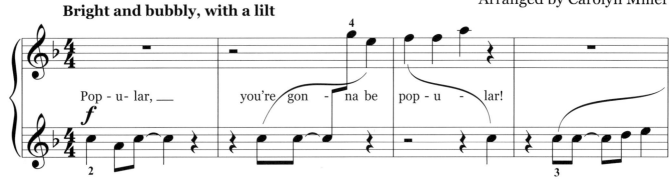

Bright and bubbly, with a lilt

Pop - u- lar, ___ you're gon - na be pop - u - lar!

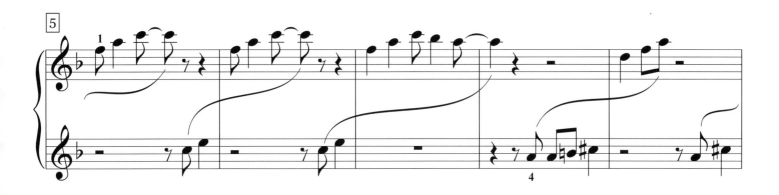

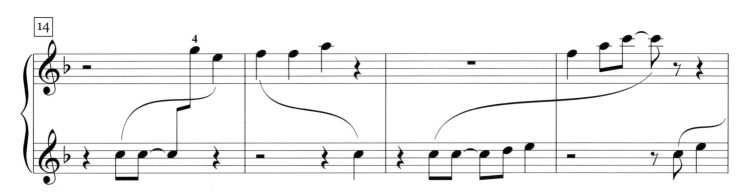

SECONDO

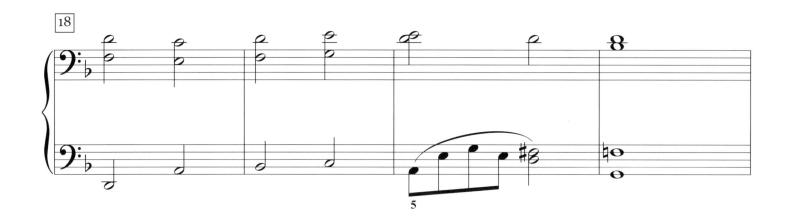

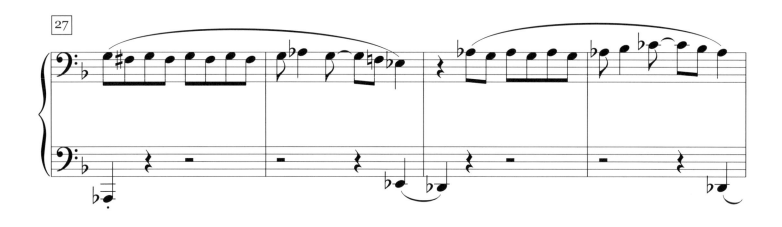

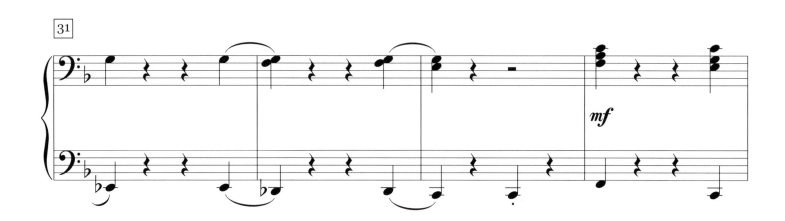

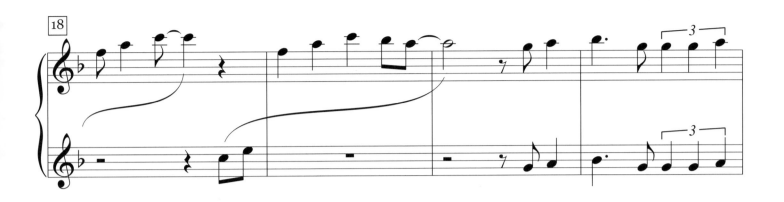

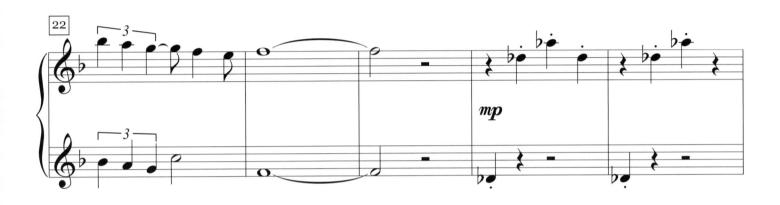

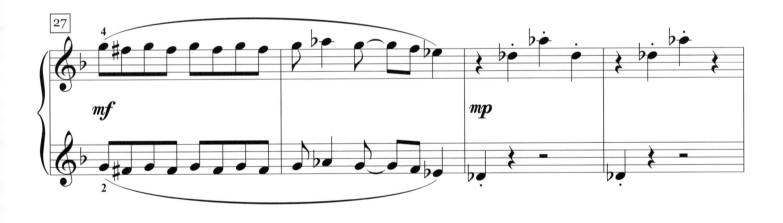

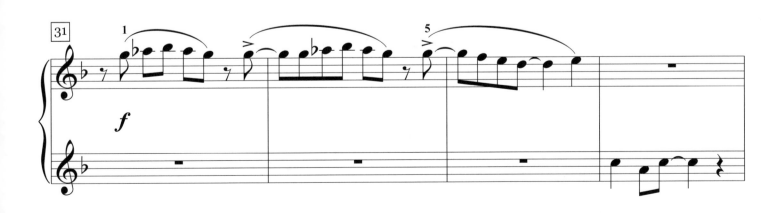

SECONDO

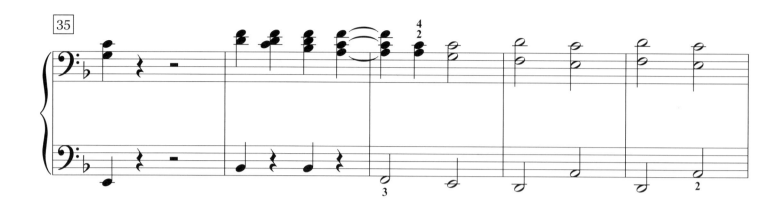

PRIMO

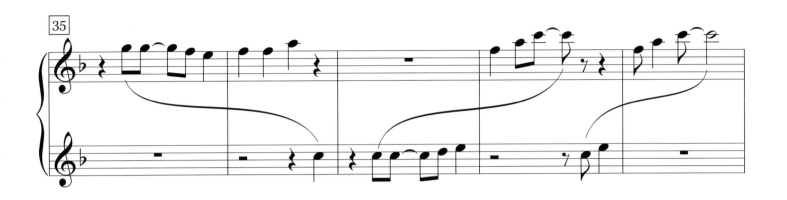

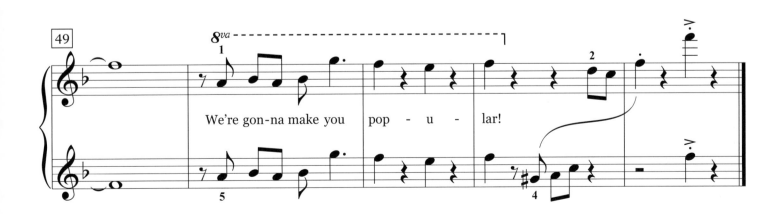

We're gon-na make you pop - u - lar!

Tomorrow
from the Musical Production ANNIE

SECONDO

Lyric by Martin Charnin
Music by Charles Strouse
Arranged by Carolyn Miller

Tomorrow
from the Musical Production ANNIE

PRIMO

Lyric by Martin Charnin
Music by Charles Strouse
Arranged by Carolyn Miller

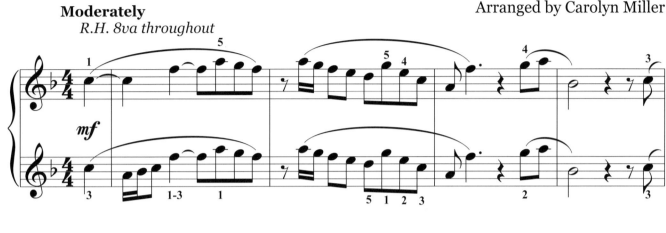

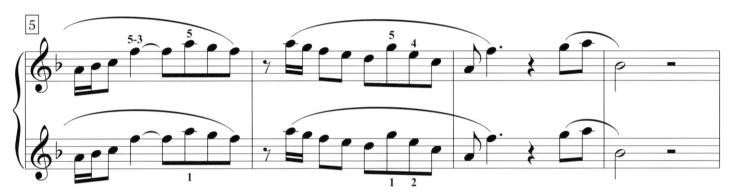

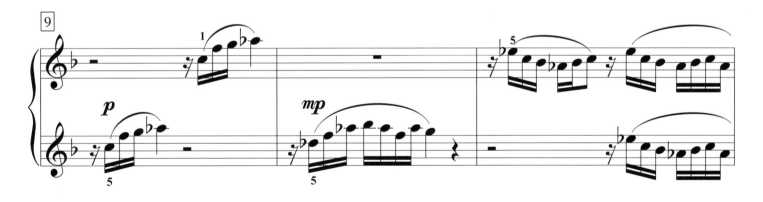

SECONDO

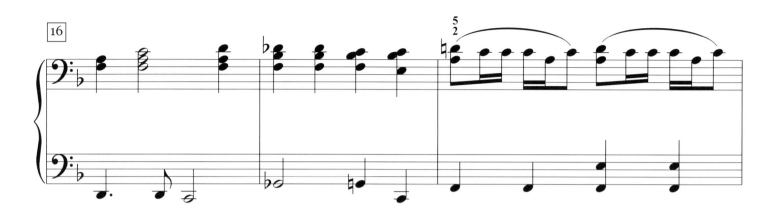

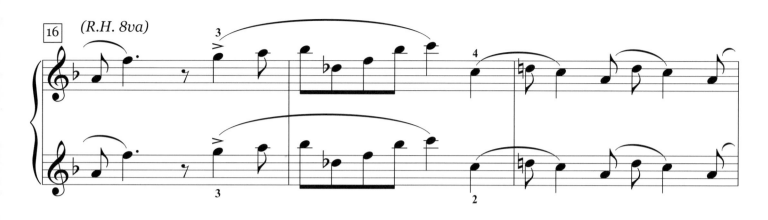

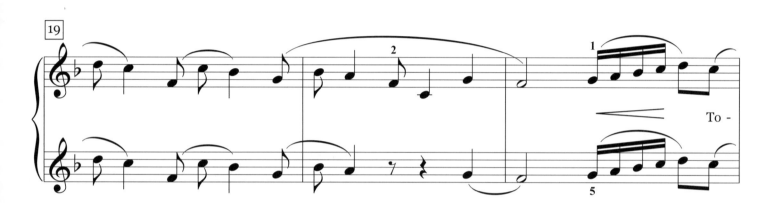

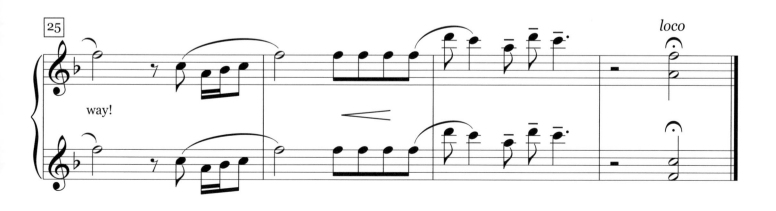

Glenda Austin is a pianist, arranger, and composer who writes piano music popular at all levels. She graduated from the University of Missouri (Columbia) with a bachelor's degree in music education and a master's degree in piano performance. Glenda has over 40 years' experience as an elementary and high school music teacher, and holds memberships in the Music Teachers National Association and Missouri Music Educators Association. A frequent adjudicator and clinician, she has presented workshops for teachers and students throughout the United States, as well as in Canada and Japan. In addition, she is collaborative pianist for the choral department at Missouri Southern State University. Married to high-school sweetheart, David, they are the parents of Susan and Scott, and grandparents of Isaac, Eden, and Levi.

Eric Baumgartner received jazz degrees from Berklee College of Music and DePaul University. He is the author and creator of Jazz Piano Basics, a series that presents jazz fundamentals in an accessible manner through short dynamic exercises. Eric is a sought-after clinician who has presented throughout the US, Canada, England, Germany, and Australia. He and his wife Aretta live in Atlanta, Georgia where he maintains an active schedule as performer, composer, and dedicated member of the local music scene.

Naoko Ikeda lives in Sapporo, Hokkaido in northern Japan, and is passionate about introducing the world to her country's essence through music. Influenced by classical music, jazz and pop, as well as the piano works of William Gillock, her own music reflects her diverse tastes with beauty, elegance, and humor. Naoko holds a piano performance degree from Yamaguchi College of Arts in Japan and currently maintains an energetic schedule as both teacher and composer.

Carolyn Miller is a teacher, pianist, and composer from Cincinnati, Ohio. She holds music degrees from the College Conservatory of Music at the University of Cincinnati and Xavier University. She has taught piano to students of all ages for many years, both private and in the classroom, and often adjudicates at music festivals and competitions. Her music teaches essential technical skills, yet is fun to play, which appeals to both children and adults. Many of her compositions appear on contest lists, including the NFMC Festivals Bulletin. Carolyn also directs a large church choir and is the pianist for special services. She enjoys spending time with her husband Gary and their entire family, especially her seven grandchildren.